# Jeff Bezos:
## Founder of Amazon and the Kindle

# Jeff Bezos:
# Founder of Amazon and the Kindle

Robert D. Scally

MORGAN
REYNOLDS
PUBLISHING

Greensboro, North Carolina

A box from Amazon.com. Amazon ships merchandise all over the world.

n.com®

d you're done.™

Business Leaders
Jeff Bezos: Founder of Amazon and the Kindle
Copyright © 2012 by Morgan Reynolds Publishing

Library of Congress Cataloging-in-Publication Data

Scally, Robert, 1958-
Jeff Bezos : founder of Amazon and the Kindle / by Robert D. Scally.
     p. cm. -- (Business leaders)
Includes bibliographical references and index.
ISBN 978-1-59935-178-0 (alk. paper) -- ISBN 978-1-59935-214-5 (e-book) 1.
Bezos, Jeffrey--Juvenile literature. 2. Booksellers and bookselling--United
States--Biography--Juvenile literature. 3. Businessmen--United
States--Biography--Juvenile literature. 4. Amazon.com
(Firm)--History--Juvenile literature. 5. Internet bookstores--United
States--History--Juvenile literature. 6. Electronic
books--History--Juvenile literature. 7. Kindle (Electronic book
reader)--Juvenile literature. 8. Electronic commerce--United
States--History--Juvenile literature. I. Title.
Z473.B47S32 2012
381'.4500202854678--dc22
[B]
                              2011015611

Printed in the United States of America
*First Edition*

Book cover and interior designed by:
Ed Morgan, navyblue design studio
Greensboro, NC

# Table of Contents

Chapter One: Jeffrey Bezos–Boy Wonder                                    9

Chapter Two: Princeton, Wall Street, and a Big Idea     25

Chapter Three: No Regrets                                                       37

Chapter Four: Amazon Gets Big Fast                                        49

Chapter Five: Creating the Kindle                                            69

Chapter Six: Beyond the Kindle                                               89

Timeline                                                                                   101
Sources                                                                                   102
Bibliography                                                                           106
Web sites                                                                               107
Index                                                                                      108

# CHAPTER 1

Rate this packaging: www.amazon.com/packaging
amazon.com®
little card
big smile™
amazongiftcards®
www.amazon.com/giftcards

# Jeffrey Bezos—Boy Wonder

When Jeffrey Bezos was three years old, he wanted to start sleeping in a real bed. His mother wanted him to stay in his crib at night. They argued about it until she came home one day to find Jeffrey taking his crib apart with a screwdriver. He got to move to the bed.

Even as a toddler Bezos displayed the tenacity he would later use to revolutionize how people shopped for books and other items, as well as how books are read.

Jeffrey Preston Bezos was born January 12, 1964, in Albuquerque, New Mexico. His mother, Jacklyn "Jackie" Gise Jorgensen, was only seventeen when he was born. She soon divorced Jeffrey's father, who played no role in Jeffrey's life.

Jackie found a job at a local bank where she met a young man named Miguel "Mike" Bezos. They fell in love and were soon married. Mike Bezos adopted Jeffrey.

Jeffrey Bezos has always considered his stepfather, Mike Bezos, to be his father. "I've never met him," Jeffrey said of his biological father. "But the reality, as far as I'm concerned, is that my Dad is my natural father. The only time I ever think about it, genuinely, is when a doctor asks me to fill out a form."

Mike Bezos was eighteen and a college freshman when he and Jackie married. But he had already over-come some major obstacles in his life. Mike was born in Cuba. As a teenager, he was taken out of Cuba as part of Operation Pedro Pan. Pedro Pan is the Spanish phrase for Peter Pan, the storybook hero who could fly. A Roman Catholic priest, Bryan O. Walsh, created

Operation Pedro Pan to take children out of Communist Cuba and give them new lives in the United States. Operation Pedro Pan was underway from December 26, 1960, to October 1962. It ended when the United States and Communist Russia came close to war over the issue of Russian missiles based in Cuba, which is just ninety miles south of the tip of the state of Florida.

More than 14,000 Cuban children were brought to the United States during Operation Pedro Pan and placed in foster care. There young Mike Bezos quickly learned English and graduated from high school in Delaware, where he lived in a Catholic mission with fifteen other Cuban refugees.

After high school, he moved 2,000 miles to the west to New Mexico where he enrolled in the University of Albuquerque. In Albuquerque, he also took a job in a bank where he met his future wife.

Despite having a young family to provide for, going to school and working full time at the bank, Mike Bezos earned an engineering degree. He went to work for the giant oil company Exxon as a petroleum engineer after he graduated, and moved the family to Houston, Texas.

In addition to his stepfather, young Jeffrey had other strong role models in his life. His grandfather, Lawrence Preston ("Pop") Gise, was one of the most important. Gise was a high-ranking government official in the U.S. Atomic Energy Commission, the agency that oversees all aspects of nuclear energy. In 1964, Gise was appointed by the U.S. Congress to manage the Albuquerque, New Mexico, regional office of the Atomic Energy Commission. He supervised 26,000 employees working at three important research centers in the western United States: the Sandia, Los Alamos, and Lawrence Livermore laboratories.

Gise was also owner of the Lazy G ranch in Cotulla, Texas, located about ninety miles west of San Antonio. Jeffrey spent many summers working and living on the 25,000-acre ranch, which his maternal ancestors, who were early settlers in Texas, had acquired over the generations. He worked hard repairing windmills, laying pipes, fixing pumps, and even castrating and branding cattle. "I spent three months every year from the age of four to the age of sixteen working on the ranch with my grandfather," he later recalled, "which was just an incredible, incredible experience. Ranchers—and anybody I think who works in rural areas—they learn how to be very self-reliant, and whether they're farmers, whatever it is they're doing, they have to rely on themselves for a lot of things."

Jeffrey's grandfather was much more than a rancher and government official. In the late 1950s, Gise had worked on space technology and missile defense systems—the kinds of things a kid growing up in the early 1970s would find very interesting. In the late 1960s and 1970s when Jeffrey was growing up, the U.S. space program was big news. Every launch and mission was broadcast on television and talked about in schools.

Apollo 11 astronaut Edwin Aldrin poses for a photo beside the U.S. flag on the Moon on July 20, 1969.

Astronauts were viewed as heroes. With the space program advancing rapidly at the time, many people assumed that soon there would be permanent bases on the moon and space stations orbiting the earth with regular flights coming and going bringing passengers from Earth. Like many young children at the time, Jeffrey began dreaming of becoming an astronaut and going into space.

Gise was very fond of Jeffrey and encouraged his interest in educational games and toys, buying Jeffrey kits to build electronics. He was always bringing home all kinds of gadgets for the boy to tinker with.

Jeffrey's mother, Jackie, also gave him technology to play with. "I think single-handedly we kept many Radio Shacks in business," she once joked.

A young boy studies an Apollo 12 rocket model in 1969.

While he was still in elementary school Jeffrey wanted an expensive electronic toy called an Infinity Cube. An Infinity Cube was a device with motorized mirrors that would enable the viewer to stare into "infinity." Jackie refused to buy it because she thought it cost too much.

This presented a challenge that Jeffrey thought he could overcome. He figured out that the toy was made of inexpensive parts that could he could easily find. So, he bought the parts and built his own Infinity Cube and in the end, he learned much more than if he had simply bought the toy. "The way the world is, you know, someone could tell you to press the button," said twelve-year-old Jeffrey. "You have to be able to think . . . for yourself."

At an early age, Jeffrey distinguished himself as someone who could think for himself both in and outside of school.

Jeffrey attended Vanguard, a special program for gifted children at Houston's elite River Oaks Elementary School. The school was part of a voluntary racial integration effort in Houston's public school system. Going to River Oaks Elementary School required Jeffrey to make a forty-mile round trip commute alone by city bus every day.

By age twelve, Jeffrey was so remarkable he attracted attention. He was the focus of a chapter in a 1977 book about educational programs for smart children in Texas. The chapter follows him through his typical day in the Vanguard program. The book offers a rare look at a child who years later would go on to do world-changing things.

Young Jeffrey is described as "slight of build, friendly but serious," "courtly," and having "general intellectual excellence." His teachers said he was "not particularly gifted in leadership," but also said he moved "confidently among his many friends."

Although his teachers may have overlooked an important part of his personality, Jeffrey thrived at River Oaks. He started reading science fiction and fantasy books. In the fourth grade, he showed his teachers how to connect to a mainframe computer over a telephone line using a modem. Then he and his friends used the computer to spend hours playing a primitive Star Trek computer game.

However, Jeffrey proved he wasn't just another computer geek. In Texas, youth sports are wildly popular and very competitive. Football is the most competitive sport of all. Although he was skinny, Jeffrey's parents signed him up for Texas youth football league. "He barely made the weight limit, and I thought he was going to get creamed out there," his mother recalled.

Instead of getting creamed, Jeffrey became the team's defensive squad captain. He was one of the few players on the team who could remember all of the plays. He not only memorized his parts in the plays, he memorized all of the player's parts for all of the plays. His intelligence and fearlessness helped make him a leader, and sports helped show his potential.

During the years he was growing up, Jeffrey's parents moved several times for his father's job. His high school years were spent in Miami, Florida.

While attending Miami Palmetto High School in Dade County, Florida, Jeffrey dreamed of becoming an astronaut, building a space station, and doing business in space. "Oh, he had ideas about space promotion!" recalled Bill McCreary, a Miami Palmetto High School science teacher. And his dream was more than just a kid's fantasy. Jeffrey took part in a high school space initiative, and he earned a trip to NASA's "space camp" in Huntsville, Alabama. Bezos won the trip for writing a report on "The Effect of Zero Gravity on the Aging Rate of the Common Housefly."

As part of their training, the Apollo 1 flight crew practices water egress procedures in a swimming pool at Ellington Air Force Base in Houston, Texas, in 1966.

To become an astronaut, Jeffrey knew he would have to excel in school. He would need top grades since NASA's astronaut program chose only the smartest candidates. So he stopped dreaming and applied himself, setting some very high goals.

Jeffrey's teen years would show that behind his easygoing manner and loud laugh was an unstoppable work ethic. This relentlessness would become one of his hallmarks at Amazon.com and in his other business ventures. When Jeffrey told his classmates about his goal of becoming class valedictorian, everyone else knew they were competing for second place, said Joshua Weinstein, a high school friend. Jeffrey was so determined that there was no way he would lose first place. "He was always a formidable presence," said Weinstein.

Jeffrey won, graduating in 1982 first in a class of 680 students. He also won a Silver Knight Award, a prestigious academic honor in south Florida schools. He had also won his school's Best Science Student award in his sophomore, junior, and senior years and the Best Math Student Award in his junior and senior years.

In his high school graduation valedictorian speech, Jeffrey promoted the idea of building outer space colonies. It was a memorable speech that provides a glimpse into Jeffrey Bezos's visionary thinking.

"He said the future of mankind is not on this planet, because we might be struck by something, and we better have a spaceship out there," said Rudolf Werner, the father of Ursula Werner, Jeffrey's high school girlfriend.

While he was working to win his academic honors, Jeffrey also worked at McDonald's. "I was

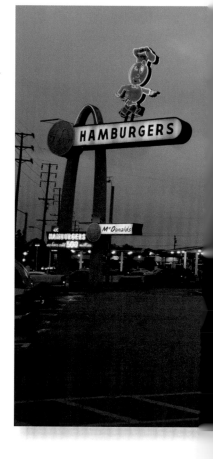

a cook," he said years later in an interview. "They wouldn't let me anywhere near the customers. This was my acned-teenager stage. They were like, 'Hmm, why don't you work in the back?' "

Jeffrey learned some valuable lessons from his job at McDonald's, including how hard work can be, how important good customer service is, and how not to get shells in cracked eggs. "One of the great gifts I got from that job is that I can crack eggs with one hand.

The oldest operating McDonald's restaurant, in Downey, California

My favorite shift was Saturday morning. The first thing I would do is get a big bowl and crack 300 eggs into it. One of the things that's really fun about working at McDonald's is to get really fast at all of this stuff. See how many eggs you can crack in a period of time and still not get any shell in them."

Working at McDonald's was also a motivating experience. Tending a greasy grill was not an experience

Jeffrey wanted to repeat. After graduation, he and his girlfriend, Ursula, came up with a business idea. This would be Jeffrey's first taste of entrepreneurship.

Ursula had just finished her freshman year at prestigious Duke University in North Carolina. She was Palmetto High's valedictorian the year before Jeffrey. During the summer of 1982, Jeffrey and Ursula were business partners in an educational kid's summer camp. They charged $150 for a two-week session geared to fifth-graders. They called their summer camp The Dream Institute.

They were able to sign up five kids, including Jeffrey's brother, Mark, and sister, Christina. The Dream Institute was run out of Jeffrey's parents' house.

Even Jeffrey's first business venture drew media attention. That summer the *Miami Herald* newspaper ran an article about the camp. Jeffrey told the paper that the camp would open "new pathways of thought" for the students, "teaching them about Jonathan Swift's book *Gulliver's Travels*, about black holes in outer space, about electric currents and nuclear arms limitations talks, about how to operate a camera."

"We don't just teach them something," Jeffrey told the *Herald*. "We ask them to apply it."

Jeffrey and Ursula broke up romantically and parted ways soon after that summer, but remained friends. He still considers her to be his first business partner.

# CHAPTER 2

Rate this packaging: www.amazon.com/packaging

# amazon.com®

little card
# big smile™

amazon giftcards·
www.amazon.com/giftcards

# Princeton, Wall Street, and a Big Idea

Bezos was accepted to Princeton University, a prestigious Ivy League college in New Jersey. Princeton graduates include presidents, successful businesspeople, and brilliant scholars. The great Nobel Prize-winning scientist Albert Einstein once taught physics there. In 1982, as a college freshman, Bezos majored in theoretical physics. He was ranked in the top twenty-five students in Princeton's honors physics program.

However, he soon discovered the competition in physics at Princeton was on a whole other level than he had seen before, and he was used to being the best at every subject.

"I looked around the room," Bezos said, "and it was clear to me that there were three people in the class who were much, much better at it than I was, and it was much, much easier for them. It was really sort of a startling insight, that there were these people whose brains were wired differently."

Bezos wasn't too shaken to learn that following in Einstein's footsteps wasn't for him. He switched his major to electrical engineering and computer science, which was then a new and rapidly growing field.

His social life flourished at Princeton. He was elected president of his fraternity, Tau Beta Pi, and was accepted into the 160-member Quadrangle Club, one of twelve elite dining societies on the university's campus. One of Bezos's future marketing executives, David Risher, was president of the "eating club." Risher recalled that Bezos liked playing "beer pong," which is similar to Ping Pong, except cups full of beer were placed on either side of the table and when a ball landed in a player's cup, he had to chug a beer. True to his love of space exploration, Bezos also joined a campus

A gallery connecting Foulke and Henry halls
at Princeton University

organization named Students for the Exploration and Development of Space.

During the summers while enrolled at Princeton, Bezos managed to land jobs that were out of the ordinary for a college student. By 1984, Bezos's stepfather's job had taken his family to Norway. That summer Bezos worked for his stepfather's employer, Exxon, as a computer programmer and analyst in the town of Stavanger, Norway. There he developed a computer program on an IBM mainframe that was used for calculating payments for oil drilling that the company owed to the nation of Norway. The following summer Bezos

View of Breiavatnet lake in central Stavanger, Norway

worked in IBM's San Teresa Research Laboratory in San Jose, California. The laboratory was located in the heart of the area known as Silicon Valley where many high technology companies are located. He was given a project estimated to take four weeks to complete. He finished it in just three days.

Bezos graduated from Princeton with honors in 1986 with an A+, a 4.2 grade point average. (Graduating with a grade point average higher than the perfect score of 4.0 is rare, but Bezos earned the score because of the overwhelming number of A-pluses he received.) For his graduating thesis, he designed and built a specialized computer for making calculations about the structure of DNA.

After graduation, several leading technology companies tried to hire him. He turned down job offers from major companies such as computer chip manufacturer Intel and the research company Bell Labs. Instead, he answered an advertisement he saw in the college newspaper. A new company called Fitel said in the ad that it was looking for Princeton's "best computer science graduates." Two Columbia University professors founded Fitel. Fitel was building a new worldwide communications network for financial trading firms. It was a start-up company and a big gamble.

He figured that at a large established company it could take years for him to reach the top. Working for a start-up he would find greater challenges that would make better use of his skills. As a young person right out of college, he felt he had nothing to lose.

Bezos was one of the first employees hired at Fitel. He quickly became head of product development and customer service. His job required him to constantly fly between New York and London, England, where the company's two offices were located.

After two years with Fitel, Bezos left for a job with the established financial firm Bankers Trust Company. At Bankers Trust, he sold software to companies that manage large retirement funds. He was promoted quickly. At twenty-six, Bezos became the youngest vice president in the eighty-year history of Bankers Trust. After two years working on the technical side of the investment business, Bezos was restless for something more challenging. He began searching for a job with a technology company that would better use his computer and math skills.

Instead, he was recruited to work at another investment company. However, this financial firm, D. E. Shaw & Co., was different. D. E. Shaw & Co. was a specialized type of financial firm known as a hedge fund. Hedge funds are investment companies that are often used by wealthy people or large companies to make the most money possible from their investments while also reducing the risk of losing money.

The company's founder, David Shaw, wanted Bezos to work on finding new types of business opportunities. Like Bezos, Shaw was a computer scientist with a Ph D in computer science from Stanford University in California, one the best universities in the United States. He specialized in inventing new ways to make money on complex financial transactions. The two liked each other instantly.

Bezos said Shaw was "one of those people who has a completely developed left brain and a completely developed right brain. He's artistic, articulate, and analytical. It's just a pleasure to talk to someone like that."

Bezos spent four years working for Shaw, starting as a vice president. Bezos's leadership ability began to show while working at D. E. Shaw. At twenty-eight, he became the company's youngest senior vice president.

"He understood how to talk about what he was doing, so that he could get other people excited about what he was doing," said former colleague Brian March. "Leadership involves, among other things, the ability to really articulate what is exciting about what everybody is working on, so that you can get everybody on board. He really understands how to do that."

While he was a rising star at D. E. Shaw & Co., Bezos was also trying to plan his personal life. Bezos's friends tried to set him up with dates. He told his friends that he was looking for a resourceful person. "The number-one criterion was that I wanted a woman who could get me out of a Third World prison," Bezos said.

He didn't meet the future Mrs. Bezos on a date set up by his friends. Instead, he fell in love with co-worker MacKenzie Tuttle. Tuttle had graduated from Princeton in 1992 and was a research assistant at D. E. Shaw. She was both smart and attractive, an aspiring writer. While studying at Princeton, she had worked as assistant to the Pulitzer Prize-winning novelist Toni Morrison. Tuttle and Bezos fell in love and married in 1993. They lived a prosperous life with an apartment on New York's upscale Upper West Side.

The next year, Bezos was put in charge of all new business ventures for D. E. Shaw. During the spring of 1994, Bezos's research found that the number of people using the Internet was growing at a rate of 2,300 percent per year. He decided that anything that fast "might be invisible today, but would be ubiquitous tomorrow."

Jeff and MacKenzie Bezos
in 2003

At the time, most people hadn't heard of the Internet. In 1990, the Internet only had about 3 million users worldwide, compared with an estimated 2 billion users today. In the early 1990s, mainly the government, universities, and scientists used the Internet. There was no such thing as Internet commerce. Going online in the early 1990s was something that was still very new.

Bezos did more research. He made lists of the twenty products he thought could be best sold on the Internet. One product kept rising to the top of the lists: books.

"You had to be able to build something that offered enough value to the customer for people to want to use this new and infant technology. Really, that meant you had to do something that could only be done online. I picked books primarily because there are so many different [titles]—there were more items in the category than in any other," Bezos said. "Over three million books are actively in print. No one could build a book store with three million titles."

Bezos showed his research to his boss. He proposed that D. E. Shaw's first Internet business should be selling books. To his surprise, his boss rejected his idea that the company could make a fortune selling books on the Internet.

It was an idea too good to let go of, Bezos thought. He knew that he could make a lot of money in Internet commerce. However, his boss, a person he respected and trusted, had shot down his big idea.

# CHAPTER 3

Rate this packaging: www.amazon.com/packaging
amazon.com®
little card
big smile™
amazongiftcards
www.amazon.com/giftcards

# No Regrets

Despite the fact that Jeffrey Bezos's plan to sell books on the Internet was rejected by his employer, he couldn't let go of the idea. It was spring 1994, and Internet use was growing at an incredible rate. Bezos kept thinking about the Internet's amazing 2,300 percent per year growth.

He didn't want to miss the chance to get into something new, exciting, and potentially profitable. He wanted to get into Internet commerce. In every way that he looked at it, books had the best chance for success as a retail business on the Internet. There were more than 3 million books in print around the world. Even the largest bookstores could have just 175,000 books on their shelves. But on the Internet, the number of book titles that could be sold was potentially unlimited. With a Web-based business, there was no need for stores with shelves where books sit taking up space. You could sell each title as people ordered them online, and then send the book to them with no need for large numbers of books on hand.

Bezos told his boss, David Shaw, that he was going to do a crazy thing: quit his job and start a business selling books on the Internet. Although Shaw admitted to Bezos that he had left a secure job at a big company to start D. E. Shaw & Co., he tried talking him out of quitting. Shaw pointed out that Bezos was making a very good living, and he had a bright future in the investment business. Shaw said that Internet book selling was a great idea, just not for someone who was already successful like Bezos.

"That logic made some sense to me, and he convinced me to think about it for 48 hours before making a final decision," Bezos recalled. While he was thinking about what to do, Bezos came up with what he called "regret-minimization framework." This was his way of saying that he wanted to make as few decisions in life as possible that he would regret later.

So he thought about the future, concluding:

> I knew that when I was eighty there was no chance that I would regret having walked away from my 1994 Wall Street bonus in the middle of the year. I wouldn't even have remembered that. But I did think that there was a chance that I might regret significantly not participating in this thing called the Internet, that I believed passionately in. I also knew that if I tried and failed, I wouldn't regret that. So once I thought about it that way, it became incredibly easy to make that decision.

Bezos talked to his wife, MacKenzie, about this idea. She agreed to give it a try.

"We had to pick a place. We wanted a place that had a large pool of technical talent, and also a place nearby a major book wholesaler," Bezos said. "It turns out the largest book warehouse in the world is in Roseburg, Oregon. We picked Seattle, because Seattle has lots of great technical talent and is close to Roseburg, so we moved."

In the summer of 1994, the couple gave up their posh Manhattan apartment. Like many New Yorkers, they didn't own a car. So they flew to Texas where Bezos's parents lived, and his stepfather gave them an old Chevrolet Blazer to make the drive west. While driving to Seattle, Bezos wrote the first draft of a business plan for what would become Amazon.com.

The first name for the company was actually created on the ride to Seattle, and it was not Amazon. The name was Cadabra, as in the magician's chant "abracadabra" just before pulling a rabbit out of a hat.

During the trip, Bezos used a cell phone to call the lawyer he was working with in Seattle. The connection wasn't good. The lawyer had a hard time hearing Bezos when he told him the name of the new company. "When I said, 'Cadabra,' the lawyer thought he said, 'Cadaver,' as in a dead body. So that name didn't last long," Bezos said.

Bezos needed a new, better-sounding name. He wanted a name that was simple, memorable, and that would give the impression that the store's selection was huge. "Probably the question I get asked most frequently

# Amazon Gets Big Fast

By 2000, the fantastic growth of the Internet had created something like the Gold Rush. Hundreds of companies hoping to cash in on the Internet's growth were planning to create new ways of doing business in what was being called "cyberspace."

As consumers flocked to the Internet, some investors were afraid that not becoming involved in some way would be a huge missed opportunity. Almost any businessperson with a plan for an online-related business—no matter how impractical—seemed to be able to find people who would give them their money. Investors poured money into these new firms, referred to as dotcoms, during the late 1990s.

This later became known as the "Internet bubble." Like an expanding bubble or balloon, the value of many Internet companies kept increasing despite the fact that many had flawed business plans and little or no revenue. Technology experts and promoters of the Internet talked of a "new economy" where the old rules of business no longer applied.

They were wrong.

Friday, March 10, 2000, is considered the day the Internet bubble burst. That day the stock exchange, where many of the new dotcom companies' shares were traded, hit an all-time high. But for the dotcom companies, it was all downhill from there. Soon the shares of these companies dropped as far and as fast as they had risen. When a recession and the terrorist attacks of September 11, 2001, slowed the economy, the Internet-related start-ups failed by the dozen.

The Internet bubble of the late-1990s is now considered an example of investors abandoning established business practices for what amounted to a fad. Similar events have happened many times in the history of financial institutions. As the twenty-first century began, e-commerce was becoming less a novelty and more of a real business. After Christmas 1999, many of the new Internet businesses failed. However, it was clear that e-commerce was here to stay and that Amazon.com was a survivor. Amazon succeeded thanks in part to Bezos's leadership, his ability to plan ahead, and his constant attention to customer satisfaction.

Today Jeffrey Bezos is a multibillionaire. He is still tall, thin, and nerdy-looking. He's balding, and what's left of his once-brown hair is gray and cropped close to the scalp. He has large hazel eyes that seem to grow bigger when he gets excited, and he gets excited a lot. He's constantly upbeat and energetic. By all accounts and appearances, he is very down-to-earth.

Bezos and his wife, MacKenzie, have four children, including a daughter adopted from China. Their first child, a son named Preston, was born in March 2000, during the height of the Internet bubble burst. Bezos once described baby Preston as "a great user-up of spare time," and "the cutest baby ever—shocking unique concept, I know!"

$1,561
Book Superstore Chain

$1,195
amazon.com

Jeff Bezos stands next to a display comparing his online company's lower book prices against a competitor while speaking at the company's annual shareholders' meeting in Seattle, Washington, in May 2003.

Some have compared Bezos's fashion sense to that of a college professor. He's often seen wearing khaki pants or blue jeans with a blue or white shirt, open at the collar. He sometimes wears a blazer for special occasions, like television appearances or speeches. He never wears a tie.

He's well known for his loud, distinctive laugh. Bezos's laugh has been compared to various animals ranging from a braying donkey to a "flock of Canadian geese." In 2000, when it wasn't yet clear the company would survive, one business publication called Bezos a "chuckling maniac" running a "terrible company."

Over the years Bezos has used his laugh to dismiss his critics and as a way of shaking off adversity. He's been described as "playing loose and goofy," a billionaire who's always able to come up with new surprises and new business to help make Amazon stand out from every other retailer.

Bezos's outward good nature hides the tougher, competitive, and more temperamental personality that only insiders see. "The thing that doesn't come off in public is that he's very hard-core," David Risher, the Princeton classmate who became an Amazon marketing executive. "There are fun moments in the four-hour meetings, but they aren't fun meetings. If someone comes in without the numbers, it can get ugly pretty quickly."

Surviving the Internet bubble came with some costs. Amazon.com's stock value dropped, drastically lowering the company's market value. To become profitable, Amazon closed some of its distribution centers and laid-off hundreds of employees. Amazon had itself invested in some other dotcom businesses, many of which failed, costing the company millions of dollars. Bezos reworked Amazon's business plan, transforming the company from a specialty retailer into something more like an online shopping mall.

The company quickly got rid of products that weren't profitable. It concentrated on improving the ways it managed its merchandise. Changes included delivering packages sorted by geography to the post office, to developing complex computer programs to figure out relationships between items that people buy so they could be grouped together in the company's warehouses.

Amazon also started selling products for other companies. It began selling products from traditional retailers such as Toys "R" Us and discount stores like Target. Amazon added merchandise from smaller retailers by creating zShops, a portion of the site where independent retailers can sell their goods. Amazon even

A Toys "R" Us store in North Bergen, New Jersey

took on online auction giant eBay with its Amazon Auctions.

The company kept growing, and its losses began to shrink during 2001 and 2002. Amazon finally turned a small profit of $35 million in 2003, its ninth year in business, and seven years after first issuing stock.

Amazon.com had survived when other Internet companies failed in the early 2000s partly because it managed to keep growing its revenues by continually adding new types of goods and services. The company's expensive investments in new technologies to improve the online shopping experience also paid off.

Once Amazon showed that it could make a profit, the company's real growth began. Amazon became the largest retailer on the Web, branching out into all kinds of products and services.

Another reason Bezos and Amazon.com managed to succeed was his plan to get big fast and then get profitable. "What few people understood was that the reason that they didn't make money was that for the previous five years every time there was a trade-off between making more money or growing faster, we grew faster," said Nick Hanauer, an early Amazon investor who convinced Bezos to move to Seattle. Amazon gave up some opportunities to make a profit so that the company would grow large enough to make it difficult for other companies to duplicate what it had done, Hanauer said.

Bezos has said that although intelligence, skill, and hard work helped to make Amazon a success, luck and timing were also on his side.

"Our timing was good, our choice of product categories–books–was a very good choice," Bezos said. When Amazon.com began, it was far from clear that people who weren't interested in playing around with computers would even use the Internet, Bezos said.

"One of the things everybody should realize is that any time a start-up company turns into a substantial company over the years, there was a lot of luck involved," Bezos said. Many entrepreneurs are very smart, very hardworking, but very few are able to achieve the kind of success that leads to a tiny little company growing into something substantial, he said.

To have the kind of success that Amazon has had requires a lot of planning, hard work, a large team of smart, dedicated people, and "it also requires that not only the planets align, but that you get a few galaxies in there aligning, too," Bezos said. "That's certainly what happened to us."

Not all of Amazon's new ventures were successful.

Bezos has been criticized for not following through on some promising business opportunities that the company paid large amounts of money to pursue. For example, in 1998 Amazon paid about $200 million for a company named Junglee. Junglee was building an e-commerce search engine, a sort of Google for products. Type the name of a certain brand of tennis shoe in the search engine, and it would find all of the Web sites where that shoe was being sold. At the same time it would show an instant price comparison between the Web sites selling that shoe. With little explanation, Bezos ended the project just eighteen months after it began. Amazon's competitor, Google, now dominates the market for online product price comparison searches on the Web.

Danny Shader worked at Amazon for fifteen months starting in 1999. Amazon bought Shader's start-up company, Accept.com, for about $200 million. Shader describes Bezos as "the smartest, best entrepreneur I've ever met in my life, and will ever meet." Shader's company had developed early online payment technology that made it possible to send money electronically to businesses or other people. But Amazon never put the kind of resources necessary into Accept.com to make it successful. PayPal, a subsidiary of Amazon's competitor eBay, is now the leading online payment company. "Quite literally we could've been PayPal if things had worked out differently," Shader said.

The PayPal home page

Bezos also has been criticized for being unable to delegate tasks to others. There are times when his focus and attention to details may have made him unable to see the bigger picture. "The good and the bad of Bezos is that he wanted to be involved with every new web site change, even if it was just to change the colors of a tab," said Brian Lent, who worked at Amazon for two years developing new technologies.

Several times during the life of the company, investors have called for Bezos to step aside and let someone who had already run companies take over. Sometimes entrepreneurs who start companies aren't the best people to run the companies once they are no longer start-ups. Some investors felt that Bezos should at least put a plan in place for someone else to step in and run the company in case something happened to him.

As one Internet start-up company after another failed in 2000, Amazon.com's stock price was falling. Some investors began asking whether Bezos was still the best person to lead the company. "Time for Bezos to Step Aside?" was the headline of one article in 2001. Gary Lutin, an investment banker, repeatedly demanded that Amazon spell out a plan for replacing Bezos.

"Jeffrey Bezos is justifiably considered a brilliant person," Lutin said. "But his brilliance has been exhibited so far in the area of stock promotion rather than running a business." Though he would later prove Lutin wrong, it wouldn't be the last time that investors would call for Amazon to make a plan for new leadership should it suddenly find itself without Bezos.

On the morning of March 6, 2003, Bezos chartered an Aerospatiale Gazelle helicopter and hired a local veteran pilot to fly over a remote mountainous area in southwest Texas. The area was near his grandfather's ranch, where Bezos had spent his boyhood summers. Now he was interested in buying his own ranch.

"We had a full cabin, and a full tank of gas, so the helicopter was heavy," Bezos recalled. "The way a helicopter takes off is to lift off a few feet, then the rotors tilt, and it needs to get some forward momentum to generate lift." But that morning powerful winds caused the pilot to nearly lose control during a takeoff. The helicopter went skidding across a field. Its main rotor hit a cedar tree. The helicopter split apart, rolled over, and wound up in shallow Calamity Creek.

The helicopter was destroyed. Fortunately its passengers, Bezos, Bezos's executive assistant, and the pilot were not seriously injured. They were able to crawl out and call for help on their cell phones. Bezos was briefly

An Aerospatiale Gazelle helicopter

# Outer Space Businessman

On the day of the accident, Bezos was looking for ranch land he could buy. Bezos had been buying ranches in the area around Van Horn, Texas, using companies that hid his identity. People involved in the real estate sales were required to sign secrecy agreements. But in 2005, Bezos spoke to the local newspaper in Van Horn and confirmed that he was buying the land to build a spaceport. When asked why he had chosen this remote area of Texas, Bezos said that he had spent summers on his grandfather's ranch in south Texas, and he wanted his family to be able to have a similar experience.

Doing business in outer space has been Bezos's dream since childhood. His dream is coming true in the form of Blue Origin, a company he founded in 2000. Blue Origin is building a manned spacecraft that will sell rides to space tourists and scientists. Bezos is even making plans for a hotel in space.

It is also Bezos's most secretive business.

Blue Origin's headquarters are in Kent, Washington, a city near Seattle. It's housed in an old warehouse that has been turned into a sleek rocket science laboratory. The company has its own rocket launch facility and a private airport located on 290,000-acres in an isolated area of southwest Texas.

It wasn't until after the helicopter crashed that existence of Blue Origin became known, and that only happened after journalists researched public documents in the state of Washington. The documents showed that Blue Origin was in the outer space business.

On November 13, 2006, Blue Origin successfully launched and landed Goddard. Goddard was the first test vehicle in the company's program known as New Shepard, which is named for Alan Shepard, one of the original seven American astronauts,

Private property signs mark Bezos's land in Texas.

and the first American to fly in space. Two more success-ful test flights took place in 2007, and in 2010 Blue Origin successfully completed a NASA contract to build a working emergency escape system for a spacecraft. It also made a special space capsule. Bezos and some other Blue Origin employees have applied for several patents on some of the reusable rocket booster technology Blue Origin is developing.

Bezos's dream of doing business in outer space wasn't something that came just from reading science fiction novels. In high school he won a trip to NASA's Marshall Spaceflight Center in Huntsville, Alabama, where he had firsthand experience with the U.S. space program. Bezos won the trip for writing a report entitled "The Effect of Zero Gravity on the Aging Rate of the Common Housefly."

hospitalized with a minor head injury. Reflecting on the accident, he later said:

> People say that your life races before your eyes. This particular accident happened slowly enough that we had a few seconds to contemplate it. I have to say, nothing extremely profound flashed through my head in those few seconds. My main thought was, This is such a silly way to die. The biggest takeaway is: Avoid helicopters whenever possible! They're not as reliable as fixed-wing aircraft.

The accident renewed calls for Amazon to make plans for a future without Bezos. But Bezos laughed off this close call, and 2003 wound up becoming Amazon's first profitable year.

From 2003 on, Amazon has remained profitable. It has kept growing and adding dozens of new businesses, some of which are very specialized. In 2006, Amazon launched a new service called Elastic Compute Cloud. Elastic Compute Cloud sells computing services to computer programmers. Another new service charges businesses to store information on Amazon.com's computers over the Internet.

Fifteen years after selling its first book, Amazon.com was still growing strong and making record profits. During 2010, a difficult year for many businesses and retailers in particular, Amazon.com made another record profit of $1.15 billion, which was nearly a third more money than the company made in 2009. It was Amazon's eighth straight profitable year.

The Longfellow Ranches, now owned by Bezos, are located in Culberson County, near Van Horn, Texas.

# CHAPTER 5

Rate this packaging: www.amazon.com/packaging
amazon.com®
little card
big smile™
amazongiftcards®
www.amazon.com/giftcards

# Creating the Kindle

In November 2007 Amazon released an e-book reader that Bezos hoped would change forever how people read books.

After three years of research and development, Amazon released the Kindle First Generation e-book reader on November 19, 2007. Kindle would do nothing less than change the course of Amazon's business and that of the entire book publishing business.

The idea of e-readers, dedicated devices for reading e-books, didn't begin with the Kindle. The first e-readers had appeared in 1993, and many more have come along since. Before the Kindle, none had been very successful. "We've been selling e-books for a long time. But nobody's been buying e-books. It's an idea that's been out there for a long time," Bezos said.

# Michael S. Hart and Project Gutenberg

Jeffrey Bezos was certainly not the first person to think of turning reading into a fully digital experience. The idea had been around almost since the beginning of the computer era. One of the most important advancements was begun years before the first Kindle was sold.

In 1994, when Bezos was first discovering the potential of the Internet, a man named Michael Stern Hart and a few dedicated volunteers from around the world had been making digital books for twenty-three years. Hart was on a mission to create a huge library of digital books that would always be available for free and readable by as many electronic devices as possible. Hart named his free digital library Project Gutenberg, after Johannes Gutenberg, a German who is credited with inventing the modern printing press in 1439. Books had previously been copied one at a time by hand. Gutenberg's printing press made it possible to mass-produce books.

Gutenberg's printing technology spread rapidly. Soon other printers in Europe were producing books using Gutenberg's technology. This allowed more people to own books. With more people owning books, knowledge spread more rapidly.

Hart hoped Project Gutenberg might have a similar effect in the digital age. From 1991 to 1996, the number of e-books compiled by Project Gutenberg doubled every year. The first Web browser, Mosaic, was released in late 1993. The development of web browsers and e-mail made it became easier for Project Gutenberg to circulate its e-books and find new volunteers.

Project Gutenberg's e-books are intentionally stored in the simplest possible way to allow them to be read on as many different types of electronic devices as possible. Hart foresees e-books eventually replacing printed text.

By 2011, Project Gutenberg offered more than 33,000 e-books in various formats for electronic devices including computers, personal digital assistants, mobile phones, smart phones, and e-book readers. It continues to grow and has numerous branches in nations around the world.

Michael Stern Hart, left, and Gregory Newby, founders of Project Gutenberg, a project to digitize public domain books as e-texts

Steve Kessel, who ran Amazon's digital-media business, pushed the idea that Amazon should build its own e-reader and helped to develop the original idea of what became the Kindle device. However, Bezos was involved in the project from the beginning. "We realized at the time that there were a few technologies that we could combine together, with the right recipe, and make something that we hoped would be transformative in the world of electronic reading," he said.

The Kindle was another example of Bezos using his drive and intelligence to invent things that could change the world. "As a young boy, I'd been a garage inventor. I'd invented an automatic gate closer out of cement-filled tires, a solar cooker that didn't work very well out of an umbrella and tinfoil, baking-pan alarms to entrap my siblings," Bezos said during his graduation speech to Princeton University's 2010 graduating class. "I'd always wanted to be an inventor."

Their aim was to invent not only a new way for people to read but also a new way for people to buy books and other publications.

"Our top design objective was for Kindle to disappear in your hands—to get out of the way—so you can enjoy your reading," Bezos said.

The idea behind the Kindle was to go beyond the physical book. The Kindle would also have several important differences from the previous generations of e-readers. For one thing, the Kindle was wireless, so whether you're lying in bed or riding on a commuter train, you can download a book and start reading it in less than a minute.

Bing Gordon, an investor and a member of the company's board of directors since 2003, said that Amazon is a company that prizes invention. The Kindle was born out of a realization that "in the future, media is not going to be sold out of a warehouse," Gordon said.

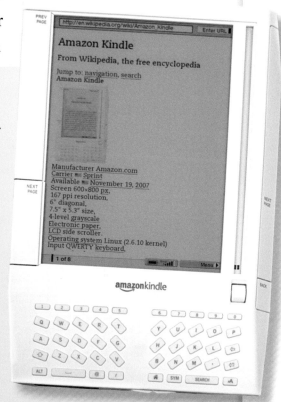

A first generation Kindle

As it had with past projects, Amazon acquired much of the talent and technology it needed to accomplish its goal of developing a new e-reader and a new way to sell e-books. The first patent for the Kindle, described as an "electronic media reader," was filed March 26, 2006, and granted on May 5, 2009, to Amazon Technologies Inc. of Seattle, Washington. The inventors were listed as Symon Whitehorn, who is a designer of high technology products, and Gregg Zehr, who is president of Lab126, a technology company owned by Amazon. Zehr led the hardware team that developed the Amazon Kindle. He had worked as an engineering executive at Apple and Palm, a maker of personal digital assistants.

Various other members of staff in the Kindle team had worked at either Apple or Palm. Whitehorn is an industrial designer. He has a background in developing electronic products.

Michael Cronan, a San Francisco-based designer, came up with the name Kindle. He had experience naming products. Cronan had also created the name Tivo, for the digital video recording device. He also designed the Tivo logo. Cronan was asked by Lab126 to name a line of electronic media readers, said Karen Hibma, Cronan's wife and business partner. "Michael came up with the name through our usual practice of exploring the depths of what the potential for the new product and product line could be and how the company wanted to present it," Hibma said.

The front of the Tivo shows the logo.

Bezos wanted to talk about the future of reading but in a way that didn't sound like bragging, Hibma said. Conan said he wanted to "give it a warm name full of potential—one that invites you to start something: 'Amazon Kindle.'" The word kindle means to set alight or start to burn, to arouse or be aroused, or to make or become bright. The word comes from an Old Norse word *kyndill*, meaning candle. The use of the word kindle to mean inspiring ideas and learning also has roots in classic literature.

"We didn't want it to be 'techie' or trite, and we wanted it to be memorable, and meaningful in many ways of expression, from 'I love curling up with my Kindle to read a new book' to 'When I'm stuck in the airport or on line, I can Kindle my newspaper, favorite blogs or half a dozen books I'm reading.'"

When the Kindle was introduced in November 2007, one magazine called it "the iPod of reading." The first production run of Kindle readers sold out in just five hours even though it cost $399, and no one had ever seen one before. Although the exact number of Kindles sold wasn't disclosed, Bezos said the rapid sellout took Amazon by surprise.

Jeff Bezos introduces the Kindle DX at a news conference in New York in May 2009.

Amazon went on to introduce new, less expensive Kindle devices. To help expand the market for its e-books and the Kindle service, Amazon gave away new software versions of Kindle reader for computers, smart phones, and electronic tablets like Apple's iPad.

Kindle evolved from being a dedicated e-book reader into an entire service that delivers books, magazines, and other printed information wirelessly with no computer or Internet connection needed. By the end of 2010, Kindle readers were Amazon's top-selling products. Amazon's sales of Kindle e-books had surpassed its sales of both hardback and paperback books.

"This is the most important thing we've ever done," Bezos said. "It's so ambitious to take something as highly evolved as the book and improve on it. And maybe even change the way people read."

There has been criticism about the way that Amazon handled the development and control of Kindle-format books. For example, Kindle books cannot be printed out. Some Kindle books cannot be read on multiple devices. Amazon also claims that readers who purchase Kindle books do not actually own those books, but have been granted a "license" to read them. This is an idea that is much different than the way paper book ownership works, and many of the related legal issues are undecided.

In July 2009, because of a dispute over distribution rights, Amazon stopped selling e-book versions of the classic novels *Animal Farm* and *1984* by George Orwell. It then deleted copies of the books that already existed on customers' Kindles and refunded the purchase price. The move angered some customers. Amazon said it changed its policies to make sure the same thing would never happen again.

Amazon's Kindle device also faces competition from other new e-readers and from a number of other devices that people can use as e-readers. The inventor of the e-book and Project Gutenberg founder, Michael Hart, has said that eventually people will read e-books, but won't buy dedicated e-readers like the Kindle.

"Why would someone spend the same amount of cash on a Kindle as on a netbook or a laptop?" Hart asked. Hart pointed out that Amazon or Sony could come out with a new model of e-reader that won't be able to read all of the books stored on the old models. He asked how long before the first Kindle and first Sony are obsolete.

Hart says that the same thing will not happen to e-books created by Project Gutenberg, which are

Bezos speaks at the annual Amazon.com shareholders' meeting in Seattle, Washington, on May 25, 2010.

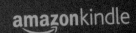

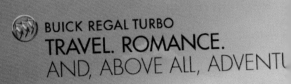

**BUICK REGAL TURBO**
TRAVEL. ROMANCE.
AND, ABOVE ALL, ADVENTU

Slide and release the power switch to wake

The Kindle e-reader

available for free from numerous sources. These e-books also existed for years before Kindle or other e-book readers came along. "The very first Project Gutenberg entry is still readable on any modern machine . . . and looks just the same now as the files downloaded on the first full day of e-book pioneering, July 5, 1971," Hart said.

Hart argues that electronic products that have a single function, like reading books, will never sell as well as products with multiple functions, like tablet computers. "So far, it would appear that e-book readers will not be a major factor in e-book reading, ever," he said.

Hart's prediction for the future of e-readers may or may not come true, but traditional publishing companies and companies that make consumer electronics also have reason to be wary of the devices. "They've seen the landscape of the previous devices, which haven't worked very well," Bezos said. That may be one reason Amazon quickly made readers available for computers, tablets, and cell phones during 2010. During a business conference in New York in 2009, Bezos spoke of the Kindle as a service, and the e-readers and e-book store as separate businesses. He also said newer versions of the Kindle would be able to read other e-book formats.

In another smart move Amazon revealed that Kindle users will soon be able to check out e-books from more than 11,000 libraries in the United State. Library lending is one of the most cited reasons many e-book users say they've opted for the Barnes & Noble Nook e-reader over the Kindle. Barnes & Noble introduced the Nook in 2009. However, with the introduction of Kindle Library Lending, which Amazon expects to make available in late 2011, Kindle users will be able to check out a Kindle book from a local library and start reading on any Kindle device or free Kindle app for Android, iPad, iPod touch, iPhone, PC, Mac, BlackBerry, or Windows Phone. Also, if a Kindle book is checked out again or that book is purchased from Amazon, all of the reader's annotations and bookmarks will be preserved. "Normally, making margin notes in library books is a big no-no," Amazon Director Jay Marine said. "But we're extending our Whispersync technology so that you can highlight and add margin notes to Kindle books you check out from your local library. Your notes will not show up when the next patron checks out the book. But if you check out the book again, or subsequently buy it, your notes will be there just as you left them, perfectly Whispersynced."

# Timeline for Development of E-books and E-readers

**1967:** Brown University professor Andries Van Dam invents the term "electronic book."

**1968:** Computer scientist Alan Kay invents the Dynabook, the prototype for today's laptops; Kay's idea leads to development of today's laptops, tablet computers, and e-readers.

**1971:** Michael S. Hart founds the Gutenberg Project, marking the start of the e-book revolution.

**1990:** The Internet has about 3 million users worldwide: most people have never heard of it.

**1992:** Charles Stack's bookstacks.com becomes the first online bookstore.

**1993:** Zahur Zapata develops the first digital book software, Digital Book v.1.; Digital Book, Inc. offers fifty digital books on a floppy disk for reading on personal computers.

**1995:** Amazon.com debuts July 16,1996; Project Gutenberg completes 1,000 titles digitized; the Internet Archive founded to create a library of digital media.

**1997:** Retail bookstore chain Barnes and Noble begins selling books on the Internet and through America Online.

**1998:** The first e-book reader, the Rocket e-book, introduced.

**1999:** Baen Books opens the Baen Free Library, offering free e-book downloads; Webscriptions starts selling unencrypted e-books.

**2000:** Stephen King book *Riding the Bullet* published in digital-only format for personal computers.

**2001:** Todoebook.com, the first Web site selling e-books in Spanish, launches in 2001.

**2002:** Book publishers Random House and HarperCollins sell digital books.

**2003:** Google begins work on Google Print and Google Book Search, later renamed Google Books.

**2004:** Sony Librie e-book reader with e-ink is introduced; Google Books is introduced; Amazon acquired Mobi pocket, a software company that makes e-book reading software for portable devices; Bookboon.com launches, allowing free textbook and travel guide e-book downloads.

**2006:** Independent e-bookstore BooksOnBoard opens, selling e-books and audio books in six different formats; Sony Reader launches; Microsoft launches Live Search Books, a search service for digitized books and scholarly articles.

**2007:** Amazon introduces the Kindle, a dedicated e-book reader that can directly download e-books from the Amazon Web site over WI-FI or a mobile network without a computer; Cybook Gen3 and PocketBook e-readers introduced in Europe.

**2008:** Adobe and Sony share e-book technologies; Sony Reader on sale in Europe; BooksOnBoard is first to sell e-books for iPhones; Microsoft ends its book-scanning project at about 750,000 books and 80 million journal articles; Google says it has scanned 7 million books; debuts "My Library" feature.

**2009:** Kindle 2, Kindle DX, and an international Kindle 2, are released; Barnes & Noble introduces the Nook e-reader; Bookboon.com reports more than 10 million downloads for the year, making it the largest publisher of free e-books; Google announces a program allowing publishers to sell digital books; in December a court stops Google from scanning copyrighted books published in France.

**2010:** Apple launches the iPad and sells more than 7 million; an optional application turns iPads into e-book readers; New Kindle 3 versions, capable of holding 3,500 books, are released; Wal-Mart sells Kindles; Google e-books (Google Editions) launches in the U.S.; Google's book scanning project passes 12 million books digitized; Google announces it will scan all known existing books by the end of the decade.

**2011:** Nook e-reader with a color screen introduced; Apple releases iPad 2; Kindle readers for Android cell phones and Windows LCD tablet computers released.

# CHAPTER 6

Rate this packaging: www.amazon.com/packaging

amazon.com®

little card
big smile™

amazongiftcards™
www.amazon.com/giftcards

# Beyond the Kindle

Bezos and Amazon.com have beaten the odds that face all new businesses. About 90 percent of all new businesses fail within five years. Thanks in part to Bezos's work ethic, resourcefulness, and good luck, Amazon.com has survived many predictions that it would fail. Of course, Amazon did much more than just survive. It became the world's largest Internet retailer.

Although the Kindle is probably Amazon's best-known recent innovation, it is one of many projects that Bezos and the company are working on. Some of Amazon's newest business ventures have nothing to do with selling books or DVDs. For example, Amazon wants to publish books, not just sell them. Amazon.com also wants to make movies, not just provide streaming video and sell DVDs.

A worker sorts packages at an Amazon.com fulfillment center.

In 2005, Amazon purchased two companies that produce customized books, audio CDs, DVDs, and downloads. CustomFlix Labs, Inc. made and distributed custom audio CDs, video DVDs, and video downloads. BookSurge offered self-publishing, on-demand printing, and online distribution for writers and book publishers. Writers could publish their own books, printing as many as they needed in small quantities.

Amazon merged the two businesses in 2009 under the name CreateSpace. The idea behind CreateSpace was to provide a one-stop service for people creating content for print, audio, and video. A writer, video maker, or musician can use CreateSpace to create customized books, DVDs, or audio CDs.

Amazon.com got into the movie business in 2010, with the goal of attracting aspiring filmmakers and screenwriters. Through Amazon Studios, Amazon offers filmmakers and screenwriters a total of $2.7 million if their projects are selected. Amazon has an agreement with film studio Warner Bros. Pictures to develop the top movie ideas and show the films in theaters. In 2011, Amazon also introduced an Internet video streaming service.

This is not the first time Amazon has gone outside its main business. During its entire history, one of the ways Amazon became successful was by continually adding new products and services.

Amazon took another big risk in 2006 when it created a service called Elastic Compute Cloud, or EC2 for short. The idea was to sell computing services to businesses. Amazon has built a vast network of computers and developed special software to power its complex Web site and the large amount of traffic it draws. As was the case in 1999, Amazon is often developing more computer capacity than it might need at any one time. So, Amazon executives decided to put the extra capacity to use and started renting out many of the things that it uses to run its own business, including its raw computing power, storage space on hard drives, and even computer software for certain types of functions.

Since introducing the service, which is now called Amazon WebServices, Amazon has almost single-handedly created a new industry. The new industry is called "cloud computing." Cloud computing is a service that provides all of the functions that might normally be found on personal computers but is instead provided over the Internet or other secure network. All of the necessary software and data storage are provided online, rather than inside a computer.

Cloud computing is so new that computer engineers can't rely on past experience while building the business. "This is not in college textbooks yet," said Lew Tucker, chief technology officer of cloud computing at technology company Cisco Systems. "These [computer] architectures are new and evolving every day."

The type of cloud computing business pioneered by Amazon has become known as "infrastructure as a service." The advantage for companies using Amazon WebServices is they don't need to buy expensive computer hardware. Amazon WebServices customers rent instead of buy the hardware for computer processing and data storage as well as the Internet services to deliver it. Amazon WebServices customers provide their own software or rent some from Amazon.

Although Amazon doesn't say exactly how much money it makes from computer services, a Wall Street investment company estimated that revenue for Amazon WebServices was about $500 million in 2010. Income from computer services was predicted to rise to $750 million in 2011, and to $2.5 billion in 2014.

A woman plays the Internet game Farmville.

Bezos said during the company's May 2010 shareholder meeting that Amazon WebServices had the potential to be as big as the firm's retail business. Given that Amazon's total sales for 2010 were $34.2 billion, Bezos's prediction for the computer services business is bold. "It's a very large area right now (and) it's done in our opinion in a very inefficient way," Bezos said. "Whenever something big is done inefficiently that creates an opportunity."

Amazon WebServices has already helped some start-up companies succeed. When Zynga Game Network launched its social-networking game Farmville in 2009 it used Amazon's computer servers to handle the rapid growth in the number of players. The number of Farmville players had far surpassed what Zynga's servers could handle. Without Amazon's computers helping out, Zynga wouldn't have been able to keep up with growth, said Mark Stockford, a Zynga vice-president. Some large companies have also used Amazon WebServices, including the New York stock exchange, digital media storage maker SanDisk, the *New York Times*, and prescription drug maker Eli Lilly.

Amazon has always been able to stand apart from its competition by introducing unique products.

Bezos at the 2010 annual Amazon.com shareholders' meeting in Seattle, Washington

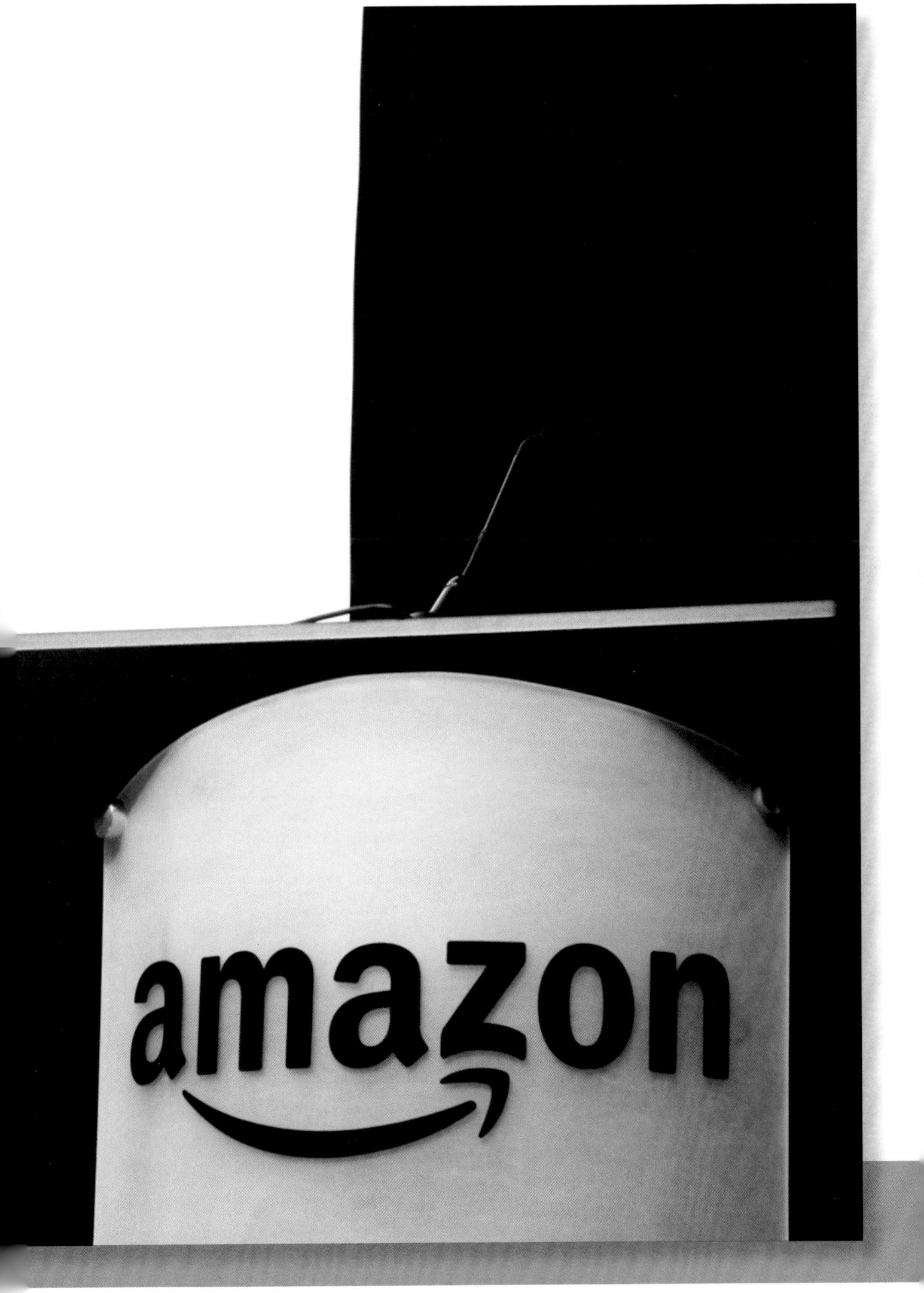
amazon

The same is true of the company's computer services business. In 2010, Amazon introduced a service called Spot Instances, which auctions off space on computer servers that Amazon isn't using. Spot Instances helped Amazon make money renting out space on servers they otherwise wouldn't have been using. Amazon's Spot Instances customers get a cheaper price for the computer services than they might have otherwise.

Another new computer services product introduced in 2011 is a service called Elastic Beanstalk. Elastic Beanstalk lets people who don't write computer code have access to Amazon's computing services.

"These guys [Amazon] continue to innovate in a way that the large traditional companies—the IBMs and the Oracles and the Microsofts of the world—are not doing," said Jeffrey Hammond, a business analyst.

Bezos doesn't waste time worrying about the competition. Who your competitors are and what they're doing has little to with running a business, Bezos said. "Whatever your set of competitors is today is transitory," he said. "You'd have to change your strategy all the time!"

What never changes for Bezos and Amazon is his focus on the company's customers. Amazon's customers want three things: the best selection, the lowest prices, and inexpensive, convenient delivery, Bezos said. "What's not going to change over the next 10 years is incredibly important—you can build plans that are durable and meet important customer needs," Bezos said. "Ten years from now, customers will still want vast selection, low prices and fast, accurate delivery."

Jeff Bezos, founder and CEO of Amazon.com

# Timeline

**1964:** Born January 12 in Albuquerque, New Mexico.

**1965:** Mother, Jackie, divorces Jeffrey's father, who plays no role in the boy's future.

**1968:** Mother marries Mike Bezos, an engineer and former Cuban refugee.

**1969:** Relocates with family to Houston, Texas.

**1982:** Attends the Student Science Training Program at the University of Florida; receives a Silver Knight Award for his academic career; graduates from Palmetto High School in Miami, Florida, as valedictorian; attends Princeton in the fall.

**1984:** Works for Exxon in Norway as a computer programmer during summer.

**1985:** Works in IBM's research laboratory in San Jose, California, during summer.

**1986:** Graduates summa cum laude from Princeton University with a BS.in computer science and electrical engineering; hired by a start-up company, Fitel.

**1988:** Hired by the Wall Street investment company Bankers Trust.

**1990:** Hired by the investment company D. E. Shaw & Co. to find new business possibilities.

**1992:** Promoted to senior vice president at D. E. Shaw & Co.

**1993:** Marries MacKenzie Tuttle.

**1995:** Amazon.com debuts July 16, calling itself "The World's Largest Bookstore."

**2000:** Son, Preston, born.

**2003:** Narrowly escapes death in a helicopter crash.

**2004:** Starts a new company centered on human spaceflight called Blue Origin; begins developing an e-book reader that eventually becomes the Kindle.

**2007:** Introduces the Kindle, a handheld electronic reading device, in November; sells out in less than six hours.

**2010:** Kindle and e-book sales reach $2.38 billion by mid-year.

**2011:** Amazon launches Kindle Library Lending, a feature that allows Kindle customers to borrow Kindle books from more than 11,000 libraries in the United States.

# Sources

Chapter One: Jeffrey Bezos-Boy Wonder

p. 10,        "I've never met him . . ." Chip Bayers, "The Inner Bezos," *Wired*, March 1999.

p. 12,        "I spent three months . . ." Daniel Alef, *Jeff Bezos: Amazon and the ebook Revolution* (Titans of Fortune Publishing, 2010), Kindle edition, chap. 1.

p. 14,        "I think single-handedly we . . ." Bayers, "The Inner Bezos."

p. 15,        "The way the world is . . ." Julie Ray, *Turning on Bright Minds* (Houston, Texas: Prologues, 1977), 47.

p. 16,        "slight of build, friendly . . . " Ibid., 42.

p. 16,        "not particularly gifted . . ." Ibid.

p. 16,        "confidently among his . . . " Ibid.

p. 17,        "He barely made the . . ." Bayers, "The Inner Bezos."

p. 17,        "Oh, he had ideas . . ." Ibid.

p. 19,        "He was always a . . ." Bayers, "The Inner Bezos."

p. 20,        "He said the future of mankind . . ." Ibid.

p. 20,        "I was a cook . . ." Charles Fishman, "Face Time With Jeff Bezos," *Fast Company*, January 31, 2001, http://www.fastcompany.com/magazine/43/bezos.html.

pp. 21-22,    "One of the great gifts . . ." Ibid

p. 22 ,       "teaching them about . . ." Sandra Dibble, " 'New Pathways of Thought' On Summer Breeze," *Miami Herald*, July 4, 1982.

p. 23,        "We don't just teach. . . ." Ibid.


Chapter Two: Princeton, Wall Street and a Big Idea

p. 26,        "I looked around . . ." Bayers, "The Inner Bezos."

p. 26,        "beer pong," Alan Deutschman, "Inside the Mind of Jeff Bezos," Fast Company.com, December 19, 2001, http://www.fastcompany.com/node/50541/print.

p. 31,        "one of those people . . ." Bernard Ryan Jr., *Jeff Bezos: Business Executive and Founder of Amazon.com* (New York: Facts on File, 2005), 22.

pp. 31-32,    "He understood . . ." Robert Spector, *Amazon.com: Get Big Fast* (New York: HarperBusiness, 2000), 18.

p. 32,        "The number-one criterion . . ." Bayers, "The Inner Bezos."

p. 32,        "might be invisible today . . ." Steve Homer, "Damn! What a Nice, Bookish Tycoon," *Independent*, November 16, 1998.

p. 34,        "You had to be able . . ." Ibid.

## Chapter Three: No Regrets

p. 39,        "That logic made some . . ." Jeffrey Bezos, "We Are What We Choose" (speech, Princeton University, Princeton, New Jersey, May 30, 2010).

p. 39,        "I knew that when . . ." *Spector, Amazon.com: Get Big Fast*, 30.

pp. 39-40,    "We had to pick a . . ." Jeffrey Bezos (speech, The Commonwealth Club of California, San Francisco, California, July 27, 1998), http://www.commonwealthclub.org/archive/98/98-07bezos-speech.html.

p. 40,        "When I said, 'Cadabra,' . . ." Ibid.

p. 40,        "So that name didn't . . ." Ibid.

pp. 40-41,    "Probably the question I . . ." Ibid.

p. 44,        "We didn't invest . . ." Joshua Quittner, "Jeff Bezos: Bio: An Eye on the Future," *Time*, December 27, 1999.

pp. 46-47,    "From a financial point . . ." Joshua Quittner, "The Charmed Life of Amazon's Jeffrey Bezos," *Fortune*, April 15, 2008.

## Chapter Four: Amazon Gets Big Fast

p. 51,        "a great user-up . . ." Matt Kelly, "Kelly's I Interview: Jeff Bezos - Q: How does it feel to be sitting on a $6bn fortune? A: I am incurably happy; MANIC GENIUS BEHIND INTERNET'S BIGGEST FIRM," *Mirror* (London, England), June 10, 2000, http://www.thefreelibrary.com/Kelly's I Interview: Jeff Bezos - Q: How does it feel to be sitting...-a062672450.

pp. 53-54,    "The thing that doesn't . . ." Deutschman, "Inside the Mind of Jeffrey Bezos."

p. 56,        "What few people understood . . ." Christine Frey and John Cook, "How Amazon.com Survived, Thrived and Turned a Profit," *Seattle Post-Intelligencer*, January 28, 2004.

p. 56,        "Our timing was good . . ." Jeffrey Bezos, interview with the Academy of Achievement, San Antonio, Texas, May 4, 2001, http://www.achievement.org/autodoc/page/bez0int-1.

pp. 56-57,    "One of the things everybody . . ." Ibid.

p. 57,        "it also requires that . . . " Ibid.

p. 58,        "the smartest, best entrepreneur . . ." Gary Rivlin, "A Retail Revolution Turns 10," *New York Times*, July 10, 2005.

p. 58,        "Quite literally we . . ." Ibid.

p. 59,        "The good and the bad . . ." Ibid.

pp. 59-60,    "Jeffrey Bezos is justifiably . . . " Carol Tice, "Time for Bezos to Step Aside?," *Puget Sound Business Journal*, May 27, 2001.

p. 60,    "We had a full cabin . . ." Quittner, "The Charmed Life of Amazon's Jeffrey Bezos."

p. 64,    "People say that your life . . ." Deutschman, "Inside the Mind of Jeffrey Bezos."

Chapter Five: Creating the Kindle

p. 69,    "We've been selling . . ." Jeffrey Bezos, interview by Charlie Rose, *The Charlie Rose Show*, November 19, 2007, http://www.charlierose.com/view/interview/8784.

p. 72,    "We realized at. . . ." Ibid.

p. 72,    "As a young boy . . . " Jeffrey Bezos, "We Are What We Choose" (speech, Princeton University, Princeton, New Jersey, May 30, 2010).

p. 72,    "Our top design objective . . ." Amazon.com, "Introducing Amazon Kindle," news release, Seattle, Washington, November 19, 2007.

p. 73,    "in the future . . . " Dan Gallagher, "Amazon's Bezos Is Anything But an Open Book," MarketWatch.com, December 7, 2010, http://www.marketwatch.com/story/Jeffrey-bezos-is-anything-but-an-open-book-2010-12-08.

p. 74,    "Michael came up with . . ." Steven Heller, "Who Named the Kindle (and Why)?,"Printmag.com/Daily Heller, December 10, 2008, http://www.print-mag.com/Article/Who-Named-the-Kindle-(and-Why).

p. 75,    "give it a warm name . . ." Michael Cronon, "A Name to Ignite an Expansive Idea," Cronon.com, undated, http://cronan.com/recent_work2.html.

p. 76,    "We didn't want it to be . . ." Heller, "Who Named the Kindle (and Why)?"

p. 77,    "This is the most . . . " Steven Levy, "Books Aren't Dead. (They're Just Going Digital.)," *Newsweek*, November 18, 2007.

p. 78,    "Why would someone spend . . ." Michael Hart, "Why The Inventor Of eBooks Says Kindle Won't Go?," Project Gutenberg News, June 1, 2009, http://www.gutenbergnews.org/20090601/why-the-inventor-of-ebooks-says-kindle-wont-go/.

p. 82,    "The very first . . ." Ibid.

p. 82,    "So far, it would . . ." Ibid.

p. 82,    "They've seen the . . . " Jeffrey Bezos, interview by Charlie Rose, *The Charlie Rose Show*, July 28, 2010, http://www.charlierose.com/view/interview/11138.

p. 83,    "Normally, making margin notes . . ." *Business Wire*, "Amazon to Launch Library Lending for Kindle Books," April 20, 2011.

p. 93,      "This is not in college . . ." Joseph Galante, "Amazon's Cloud-Computing Guru Honed Skills Fixing Lamborghinis," *Bloomberg BusinessWeek*, February 9, 2011.

p. 95,      "It's a very large area . . ." Nick Clayton, "Meet the Rainmakers," *Wall Street Journal*, February 15, 2011.

p. 98,      "These guys [Amazon] continue . . ." Galante, "Amazon's Cloud-Computing Guru Honed Skills Fixing Lamborghinis."

p. 98,      "Whatever your set . . ." Quittner, "The Charmed Life of Amazon's Jeffrey Bezos."

p. 99,      "What's not going . . ." Ibid.

# Bibliography

Alef, Daniel. *Jeffrey Bezos: Amazon and the eBook Revolution*. Santa Barbara, California: Titans of Fortune Publishing, 2010.

Daisey, Mike. *21 Dog Years: Doing Time @ Amazon.com*. New York: Free Press, 2002.

Marcus, James. *Amazonia: Five Years at the Epicenter of the dot.com Juggernaut*. New York: NewPress, 2004.

Ray, Julie. *Turning on Bright Minds*. Houston, Texas: Prologues, 1977.

Ried, Robert H. *Architects of the Web: 1,000 Days that Built the Future of Business*. New York: John Wiley, 1997.

Kalpanik, S., Neha Talreja, and Dr. Colin Zheng. *Inside the Giant Machine, An Amazon.com Story*. Seattle, Washington: Center of Artificial Imagination, 2010.

Spector, Robert. *Amazon.com: Get Big Fast*. New York: HarperBusiness, 2000.

# Web sites

**http://www.amazon.com/**

Home page for Amazon.com, the world's largest Internet retailer.

**http://www.blueorigin.com/**

Home page of Jeffrey Bezos's spacecraft design company.

**http://www.charlierose.com/view/interview/11138**

Jeffrey Bezos interviewed by public television talk show host Charlie Rose in July 2010. Bezos discusses the Kindle and its future.

**http://electronics.howstuffworks.com/gadgets/travel/amazon-kindle.htm/ printable**

An article describing in detail how a Kindle e-reader works and what kinds of electronic parts are inside.

**http://www.gutenberg.org/wiki/Main_Page**

Home page for Project Gutenberg, the original effort to create and distribute free e-books. More than 33,000 e-books that can be read on all electronic devices are available for download free.

**http://mitworld.mit.edu/video/417**

An hour-long keynote speech and interview with Jeffrey Bezos at the Emerging Technologies Conference at the Massachusetts Institute of Technology, September 27, 2006.

# Index

Accept.com, 58
Amazon.com, *4-5*
    beginnings, 34, 39-40
    business plans, 44, 54
    company name, 40-41
    computing services, 92-93, 95, 98
    deficiencies, 57-59
    early years, 42-43
    future plans, 90-93, 95
    growth of, 44, 55-56
    investors, 40, 59-60, 73
    leadership of, 59-60
    products and services, 44, 54, 56, 90-93, 95
    profits, 44-45, 55-56, 64-65, 93, 95
    stocks, 43, 54-55, 59
    success of, 43, 57, 89
    warehouses, 46-47, *90*
Amazon Studios, 91
Amazon WebServices, 92-93, 95

Baen Free Library, 85
Bankers Trust Company, 30
Barnes & Noble, 83, 85, 87
Bezos, Jacklyn Gise Jorgensen (mother), 9-11, 14-15, 40, 42, 44
Bezos, Jeffrey Preston, *33, 45, 52, 76, 79, 96, 100*
    accident, 60, 64
    as an entrepreneur, 22-23, 57, 59
    business intuition, 46-47, 51
    business ventures, early, 19, 22-23
    character, 10, 15-17, 19, 29, 31-32, 39, 51, 53-54, 59, 72
    childhood and youth, 9-14, 16-17, 19-23, 72
    college years, 25-26, 28-29
    and computers, 28-32
    education, 15-17, 19-20
    honors and awards, 19, 26, 29-31, 45
    marriage and family, 32, 51
    real estate investments, 62-63, *63, 66-67*
    social life, 26, 32
    space, interest in, 13, 17, 19, 20, 26, 28, 62-63
    technology, interest in, 14-16
    work ethic, 12, 19-20, 89

Bezos, MacKenzie (wife), 32, *33,* 39-40, 44
Bezos, Mike (father), 10-11, 28, 40, 42
Blue Origin, 62-63
bookboon.com, 87
Bookpages.co.uk, 44
books, selling online, 34-35, 38, 56, 69-70, 72
BooksonBoard, 86
bookstacks.com, 84
BookSurge, 91

CDNow, 44
Cisco Systems, 93
cloud computing, 64-65, 92-93
CreateSpace, 91
Cronan, Michael, 74-75
customer service, importance of, 20, 51, 98-99
CustomFlix Labs, Inc., 91
CyBook Gen3 e-reader, 86

D. E. Shaw & Co., 30-32, 34, 38-39
Digital Book Inc., 84
digital books, 70-71
dotcom companies, 50-51, 54
Dream Institute, 22-23
Dynabook, 84

eBay, 58
e-books, 69-71, 74, 77, 82-87
e-commerce, 34-35, 37-38, 44-47, 49-51, 54, 55, 57-58
Elastic Beanstalk, 98
Elastic Compute Cloud (EC2), 64-65, 92
e-mail, 70
e-readers, 72-74, 78, 82-87

Farmville, *94,* 95
Fitel Company, 29-30

Gise, Lawrence (grandfather), 11-14, 60, 62
Goddard (space vehicle), 62-63
Google, 57-58, 86, 87
Google Books, 85
Gordon, Bing, 73
Gutenberg, Johannes, 70

Hanauer, Nick, 56
HarperCollins, 85
Hart, Michael S., 70-71, *71*, 78, 82, 84
Himba, Karen, 74-75

Internet, growth of, 32, 34, 37, 39, 49-51
Internet Archive, 84
Internet Movie Database, 44
iPad, 77, 87

Junglee, 57-58

Kay, Alan, 84
Kessel, Steve, 72
Kindle e-reader, 69, 72-78, *73, 76, 80-81,* 82-83, 90
Kindle Lending Library, 83

Lab126, 74
Lent, Brian, 59
libraries and e-books, 83
licensing of Kindle e-books, 77-78
Live Search Books, 86
Lutin, Gary, 59-60

March, Brian, 31
Marine, Jay, 83
McCreary, Bill, 17
Mobi pocket e-reader, 85
Mosaic (web browser), 70

Newby, Gregory, *71*
Nook e-reader, 83, 87

on-demand printing, 91

PayPal, 58, *58*
Pocketbook e-reader, 86
Project Gutenberg, 70-71, 78, 82, 84

Random House, 85
Risher, David, 26, 53
Rocket e-book, 85

self-publishing, 91
Shader, Danny, 58
Shaw, David, 31, 34-35, 38
Shepard, Alan, 62-63
Sony Librie e-reader, 85
Sony Reader, 86
space programs, 13-14, 62-63
Spot Instances, 98
Stack, Charles, 84
Stockford, Mark, 95

Target, 54
Toys "R" Us, 54, *55*
Tucker, Lew, 93

Van Dam, Andries, 84

Warner Bros. Pictures, 91
Webscription, 85
Weinstein, Joshua, 19
Werner, Ursula, 20, 22-23
Whitehorn, Symon, 74
wireless internet, 73, 77, 86

Zapata, Zahur, 84
Zehr, Gregg, 74
zShops, 54
Zynga Game Network, 95

# Photo Credits